DATE DUE

Leder, Jane

Soccer

• LEARNING HOW •
Soccer

BY
JANE MERSKY LEDER

Bancroft-Sage Publishing
601 Elkcam Circle, Suite C-7, P. O. 355   Marco, Florida 33969-0355 USA

• LEARNING HOW •

Soccer

AUTHOR
JANE MERSKY LEDER

EDITED BY
JODY JAMES

DESIGNED BY
CONCEPT and DESIGN

PHOTO CREDITS
Alan Leder: Cover, Pages 5, 6, 9, 11, 12, 13, 15, 17, 19, 20, 21, 22, 23, 24, 25, 26, 27, 29, 30, 33, 34, 37, 38, 39, 40, 42.
Wide World Photos: Page 44.
Concept and Design: Pages 8, 11.
The Bettman Archive: Page 7.

ACKNOWLEDGMENTS
Special thanks to Fred Dressler, Dick Ginsberg, Hubert Krueger, Carol Maliza and all AYSO players, coaches, and parents for their cooperation, patience, and expertise. The weather wasn't always perfect, but your sterling spirits pulled us through.

TABLE OF CONTENTS

LIBRARY OF CONGRESS
CATALOGING-IN-PUBLICATION DATA

Leder, Jane Mersky.
  Learning how: soccer / by Jane Mersky Leder; edited by Jody James; illustrated by Concept and Design.
    p.   cm. – (Learning how sports)
  Summary: Examines the history, rules, techniques, and equipment of soccer.
ISBN 0-944280-32-3 (lib. bdg.) – ISBN 0-944280-38-2 (pbk.)
  1. Soccer – Juvenile literature. [1. Soccer.]   I. Title.
GV943.25.L43   1992
796.334–dc20

91-22937
CIP
AC

**International Standard
Book Number:**
Library Binding 0-944280-32-3
Paperback Binding 0-944280-38-2

**Library of Congress
Catalog Card Number:**
91-22937

INTRODUCTION

The players on both teams have waited all year for this moment. They are playing in a championship soccer game. The score is tied 1-1.

There is only one minute left in the game. Parents, friends, and coaches are cheering for their favorite team. The seconds are ticking away. Players on the field are doing their best.

The referee looks at his watch. Only thirty seconds left . . . suddenly, a player dribbles the ball down the side of the field. He dribbles past two players on the other team. He is getting closer to the goal. Fans are yelling, "Go! Go!" Everyone is excited. Will he score?

Time is running out. The player with the ball moves closer to the goal. He can see the goalkeeper watching him. Now is the time to think and act fast. The fans are cheering.

The player with the ball bends his right knee and brings his right foot back. He spreads his arms to keep his balance. Then . . . boom! He kicks the ball as hard as he can. The ball flies through the air.

The goalkeeper sees it coming toward him. He jumps to his right to catch it. But the ball sails over his head and into the goal. The Bombers have won the game! They are the new champions.

Soccer is a fun game to play and an enjoyable game to watch.

CHAPTER ONE:

The Game of Soccer

Soccer is one of the most popular sports played by young people. There are more than 25,000 American Youth Soccer Organization (AYSO) teams in 38 states, Washington, D.C., and Puerto Rico.

Soccer is an exciting and popular sport played by young people.

Contrary to popular belief, soccer has been played in the United States longer than baseball, football, or basketball. In 1869, two college teams, Princeton and Rutgers, played what people have said was the first American football game. But the game was really a soccer match. It was soccer that gave birth to football and to rugby, not the other way around. And when Dr. Naismith invented basketball, he used an old peach basket and a soccer ball!

Soccer is like these other sports in many ways. Like hockey, soccer has a goalkeeper. Like basketball, soccer has players that run up and down the field (court). And like football, soccer has defensive and offensive players. But soccer is its own game. It has its own rules. And it has its own special skills.

Soccer was the forerunner to the game we now know as football.

The Field

Soccer is played by two teams on a field about the size of a football field—100 to 130 feet long and 50 to 100 feet wide. (Smaller fields may be used for younger players). The field is divided into halves. A center circle at the half-line is used for **kickoffs**.

Each end of the field contains a goal area and penalty area. The penalty area is a box-shaped area in front of the goal posts, where the goalkeeper plays.

Arcs (like quarter circles) are marked in each corner. From these arcs, **corner kicks** are taken each time the **defensive team** kicks the ball over its own **goal line**. The ball is placed in the arc nearest to where the ball went out of play. A member of the **offensive team** kicks the ball back into play.

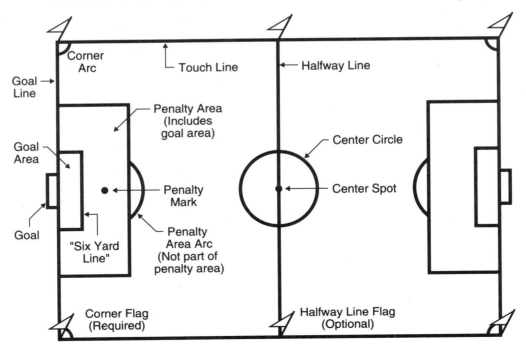

Scoring

The main objects of soccer are to score in the other team's goal area and to stop the other team from scoring in your goal area. Each **goal** is worth one point. At the end of the game, the team with the most points wins. To score, a team must put the ball between the **goal posts** and under the crossbar. The entire ball must cross over the goal line. A player may kick the ball or use any part of the body, except the hands and arms, to score. Using any part of the hands or arms causes a penalty to be called.

To score, a team must put the ball between the goal posts and under the crossbar.

Positions

Each team has eleven players on the field at any one time. The four main positions are the **forwards, midfielders** (or halfbacks), **defenders** (or fullbacks), and the **goalkeeper**.

The main job of the forwards is to score. Forwards should be good "shooters." That is, they should be able to kick the ball quickly and accurately. They should be fast and should know how to dribble the ball well.

The main job of the midfielders is to help the forwards score by getting the ball and passing it to them. The midfielders play both offensively and defensively. They link the forwards with the defenders.

As you might expect, the main job of the defenders is to keep the other team from having a good shot at the goal. Defenders also work to get the ball away from the opposing team. When the defenders get the ball, they pass it to a teammate to start an attacking play. Defenders must be able to handle and control the ball, especially in front of their goal. The defenders must keep moving with the play, like a wave or water in a bathtub. They usually can see the play developing in front of them on the field and know where the ball is going.

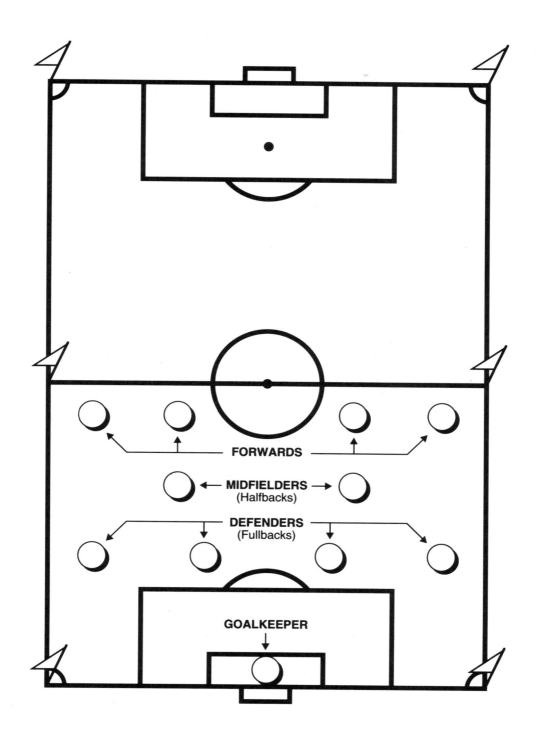

FORWARDS

MIDFIELDERS
(Halfbacks)

DEFENDERS
(Fullbacks)

GOALKEEPER

The goalkeeper's job is to keep the ball from going into the goal when the other team shoots. The goalkeeper is the only player on the field who can use hands or arms to catch the ball or block it. Good goalkeepers talk to their defenders. The goalkeeper directs the defense and tells the players where to go. A good goalkeeper learns how to cut down the angle of the ball by moving away from the goal line and toward the person who is going to shoot the ball. That makes it harder for the shooter to score a goal. The goalkeeper also has to be able to kick or throw the ball accurately for long distances after the ball stops.

The goalkeeper is the only player on the field who can use hands or arms to catch the ball or block it.

The goalkeeper directs the defense and tells the players where to go.

Teamwork

On the best soccer teams, all the players work together. It takes all eleven players to win a game. One player cannot do it alone. Every player is important. When a player keeps the ball, or does not pass it to an open teammate, that player hurts the team. Don't try to win a game by yourself. Soccer is a team sport.

It is important for players to talk to each other during a game. This helps each player know what the others are doing. If the ball is coming to you, tell your teammates that you are ready for it. If you are the goalkeeper, tell your teammates where the ball is headed and where they should go. For example, the goalkeeper will tell a player, "Move to your left," or "Watch Number Nine." The more you and the other players talk, the better you will play.

Every member of the team can help score. Many "drives" begin when the goalkeeper gets the ball. The goalkeeper kicks or throws the ball to his or her team's defenders or midfielders. They then pass the ball until they get it to one of their forwards who is in the right place to score.

When members of the other team get the ball in their own territory, your forwards become defenders, too. The forwards, along with the other players, try to take the ball away. If one of your team's defenders gets the ball, he or she passes it to the midfielders or forwards. They then start another attack on the opposing team's goal.

Soccer is a team sport and all players must work together.

CHAPTER TWO:

Basic Soccer Skills

There are five basic soccer skills that every player needs to learn. The more you practice each skill, the better player you will be.

Kicking

Kicking is the skill used most often to move the ball from one player to another or to score a goal. With the knee of the kicking leg bent, bring your foot back. Then, kick the ball very hard with the side of your foot. Make sure that you follow through with your foot. It is important not to cut the swing short but to swing all the way through. Kicking the ball in soccer is a lot like swinging a golf club or swinging a baseball bat. It is important to keep your eye on the ball.

Kicking a soccer ball requires both power and accuracy. If you kick a ball toward the goal or to another player accurately but with no power, the goalkeeper can stop it easily or a player on the opposing team can intercept it. If you kick the ball hard but with no accuracy, it will not go where you want it to go. You may accidentally kick it right to the goalkeeper or to an opposing player. The best way to kick the ball accurately is to kick it with the inside of your foot.

Kicking a soccer ball requires both power and accuracy.

There are many ways to practice kicking a soccer ball. You can practice with other players or by yourself. Some soccer coaches think it is a good idea to go to a park or playground with friends and just kick the ball around. If you play on a team, your coach will set up some kicking drills. For example, the coach may create a goal between orange cones and ask you to kick the ball between them. This may help you improve the accuracy of your kick.

One way to practice kicking by yourself is to find a high wall against which you can kick. Place a mark on the wall with masking tape. Put the ball about ten feet away from the wall and kick the ball toward the mark. Practice kicking the ball with your right foot and then with your left foot. When you can hit the mark most of the time, move fifteen feet away, then twenty feet.

It is also important to know how to kick a bouncing ball. A coach or friend can bounce the ball to you, or you can throw the ball up in the air or against a wall so that it bounces. The important thing is to kick the ball while it is on its way down, not while it is on its way up.

Kicking is an important skill to learn. In fact, forwards usually take five or six shots at the goal during each game. But you must learn the other skills, too. That way, you will be an all-around player.

Soccer coaches suggest that beginning players should practice kicking the soccer ball at a park or playground with friends.

Kicking is a very important skill to learn if you are going to play soccer.

Passing

Passing is a term for kicking, pushing, or heading (moving the ball with your forehead) the ball accurately to a teammate or to a space where a teammate can run to the ball. A player may pass the ball down the field or to a teammate several feet away.

Before you pass the ball, you must decide where you want the ball to go. Once you know where you want to pass, you must think about the right way to move the ball.

The most accurate way to pass is to use the large, flat part of the inside of your foot. Using the middle part of your foot gives you more control. Point that part of your foot out so that the inside of the foot is forward.

Raise your foot off the ground, even with the center of the ball. Then swing your foot forward so that it hits the center of the ball. Follow through in a straight line.

When passing the ball, you must decide where you want it to go, then the right way to move the ball.

You should learn to pass with both feet. At first, you can pass the ball to a friend or to a teammate close to you. When you feel comfortable, you can try passing to someone further away.

Use the large flat part of the inside of your foot to pass accurately.

Follow your pass through in a straight line.

The inside-of-the-foot pass is the most important pass for most players. However, there is another pass you may want to learn. It is called the **chip pass** or short chip pass. The idea is to kick the ball over a defender's head to your teammate on the other side of the defender.

To make a chip pass, you kick the ball with the top, flat part of your foot, where your toes end. First, get your foot under the ball. Then swing with the lower part of your kicking leg. The ball should go six to eight feet in the air.

The idea of a chip pass is to kick the ball over a defender's head to a teammate on the other side of the defender.

A good way to learn the chip pass is to have someone roll the ball to you. Make sure your toes are on the ground and that your heel is off the ground. Let the ball roll up your foot. Then lift your foot in the air about two inches. The ball should come up about chest high. After that, have the ball rolled to you and practice a complete chip pass. This time, the ball should go six to eight feet in the air.

A ball that has had a good chip pass should go six to eight feet in the air.

Dribbling

In basketball, players dribble the ball with their hands. In soccer, players dribble the ball with their feet. In both sports, the players run while they move the ball.

Dribbling is a method of moving the ball down the field using only your feet. Soccer players dribble the ball down the field when no players from the other team are nearby. Players can also dribble to get past an opponent when no teammates are open to receive the ball.

Players dribble the ball with a lot of little kicks: kick...run...kick...run. It is important to keep the ball close to you. If you kick the ball with too much force, an

When dribbling the ball down the field, you use only your feet.

opponent can kick it away. If you kick the ball with too little force, you won't be able to run fast enough.

You can use the insides or the outsides of your feet to dribble the ball. When you use the inside of your foot, kick with the side of your big toe. When you use the outside of your foot, kick with the base of your little toe.

When a basketball player dribbles, he or she looks down the court, not down at the floor. When you are dribbling a soccer ball, the same idea applies. You need to see where your opponents are and find out if any of your teammates are open to receive a pass.

It is important to keep the ball close to you when dribbling so your opponent can't kick it away.

If you are dribbling and an opponent starts to **charge** you, pass the ball to a teammate. If no teammates are around, you may have to dribble around your opponent. You can do this by speeding up and dribbling around and past the opponent. The change in your speed may fool the opponent and give you space and time for your next move.

The more you practice dribbling, the better you will be. You will learn how to change direction quickly. You may learn how to come to a sudden stop by putting your foot on top of the ball. "Faking out" your opponents is a good way to keep the ball and move closer to the goal.

The more you practice dribbling, the better you will be able to change direction quickly and "fake out" your opponent.

Trapping

Trapping is a term for stopping the ball in the air or on the ground. It prevents the ball from going past you. Once you trap the ball, you get control of it. Then you can either dribble it or pass it to a teammate.

You can trap a low ball with your foot.

You can trap the ball in many ways. You can let the ball hit your chest so that it drops to the ground. You can trap the ball with your thigh or with a bent knee. Or, you can use your foot to trap the ball.

It is important to remember that you cannot use your hands or arms to stop the ball. That means you have to keep your hands away from the ball. If you trap the ball with your hands or arms, you will get a penalty.

When you trap a low ball with your foot, the ball stops between the bottom of your foot and the ground. To trap a high-kicked or high-bouncing ball with your chest, use the middle of your chest, just above your stomach. When you trap a steeply falling ball with your thigh, use the flat part of your upper leg to stop the ball.

After you trap a ball with your foot, chest, or thigh, you need to control it. By using your body correctly, you can deaden the ball when it hits you so that it drops to the ground near you. Then you can decide whether to dribble the ball down the field or pass it to a teammate.

When you trap a steeply falling ball with your thigh, use the flat part of your upper leg to stop the ball.

Heading

Heading is a way of moving the ball by hitting it with your forehead. When a ball is too high to kick, you can "head" the ball to pass it to a teammate or score a goal.

The right way to head the ball is to keep your eyes open and your mouth closed. As the ball flies toward you, hit the ball with your forehead. You do not need to worry about hurting your forehead if you hit the ball properly. The forehead is a very hard part of the body. Do not let the ball hit you. *You* hit *it!*

Some soccer coaches use a beachball to teach heading. As the players get better at heading, they start using harder balls.

When a ball is to high to kick, you can "head" the ball to pass it to a teammate.

CHAPTER THREE:

Soccer Action

There are several ways to put the ball in action in a soccer game. The kickoff, throw-in, and several types of kicks are used. The type of action depends on why the ball is not in play. This chapter explains when and why each method is used.

The Kickoff

The kickoff is the way a team puts the ball into play at the beginning of each half of the game and after each goal is scored. The referee puts the ball on the **half-line** in the center of the field. Each team must stand on the side of the half-line they are defending. Usually, the winner of a coin toss gets a choice of kicking off or picking which goal to defend.

The kicker cannot touch the ball a second time until it is touched by another player. The ball must be kicked at least two feet before play can begin.

The Throw-In

When a player on the other team dribbles, passes, or kicks a ball out of bounds across a sideline, your team gets a **throw-in**. A player on your team throws the ball in from the point where it went out of bounds.

To take a throw-in, keep both feet on the ground behind the sideline. Hold the ball with your hands slightly behind it and put both hands straight up and behind your head. The ball should touch the back of your neck. Then bring the ball back over your head and release it.

When a player throws in the ball, that player may not touch it again until another player on either team touches it first.

The faster you can take the throw-in, the better. You can sometimes catch the other team napping and take advantage of them not being ready. Then your team can dribble or pass down to the other team's goal and shoot.

A throw-in can be a very good way to score a goal. It is important to practice throw-ins and work out different plays.

Goal Kick

A **goal kick** is a free kick taken by the defending team when the attacking team kicks the ball out of bounds across the goal line. (A throw-in is taken when the ball is kicked out of bounds across a sideline.)

The ball is placed anywhere inside the goal area. A player must kick the ball past the penalty box before it is in play again.

A defender might kick the ball just outside of the penalty box to a teammate who then taps it back to the goalkeeper. Then the goalkeeper picks the ball up and kicks it down the field.

When a goal kick is taken, a player must kick the ball past the penalty box before it is in play again.

Corner Kick

When the defensive team kicks the ball **out of play** across the goal line, the **attacking** team gets a corner kick. The ball is put within the three-foot arc in the corner of the field nearest to where the ball went out of play. A member of the attacking team kicks the ball into play. The kicker should try to kick the ball in the air toward the edge of the goal box.

The goalkeeper and several defenders on the other team should protect their goal on a corner kick. If they are not careful, the kicker or one of the forwards can easily score a goal.

When making a corner kick, the ball is put within the three-foot arc in the corner of the field where the ball went out of play.

Fouls and Penalties

The rules of soccer make the game safe and fair. If a player breaks a rule, the **referee** calls a **foul** and a **penalty kick** is awarded.

A **penalty** is a free shot at the goal. Only the goalkeeper is allowed between the kicker and the goal. A penalty is awarded when a defending player makes a major or minor foul in his or her own **penalty box**. There are two types of penalty kicks: the direct free kick and the indirect free kick.

Penalty Kick: A Direct Free Kick

When the penalty kick is awarded, the referee places the ball on the spot where the foul was made—this must be twelve yards away from the goal line. The referee then whistles for an attacking team player to move directly to the ball and kick it in an attempt to score. All other players must be at least ten yards from the ball and outside the penalty area. The goalkeeper must stand on the goal line between the posts without moving his or her feet before the ball is kicked. Once the ball is kicked, the goalkeeper tries to stop it from going into the goal.

The best way to shoot a penalty kick is with the inside of the foot. It is important to look at the goal and to know where you are going to put the ball.

When you shoot, aim the ball at the lower corner of the goal. If you just kick it as hard as you can to the center of the goal, the goalkeeper will probably save it every time.

Table A-1 shows the nine major fouls in soccer that result in a **direct free kick.**

Table A-1: Major Fouls

kicking	kicking at an opponent, whether or not contact is made
tripping	tripping an opponent, whether or not the player falls down
holding	using hands, arms, or any part of the body to stop the progress of an opponent
jumping at	jumping at an opponent with the idea of slowing the opponent down
charging violently	violent shoulder-to-shoulder contact
strike	striking or trying to strike an opponent
charging from behind	running into an opponent from behind
pushing	pushing an opponent
handling the ball	using any part of the hand or arm intentionally to direct the movement of the ball

When making a penalty kick, the referee places the ball on the spot where the foul was made - twelve yards away from the goal line.

The goalkeeper must prevent the penalty kick from going into the goal.

Penalty Kick: An Indirect Free Kick

An **indirect free kick** penalty is awarded when a minor foul is made. On an indirect free kick, at least one other player besides the kicker must touch the ball before it goes into the goal. (On a direct free kick, only the kicker has to touch the ball before it goes into the goal.) Table A-2 shows the five minor fouls that result in an indirect free kick.

When a minor foul is made, an indirect free kick penalty is awarded.

Table A-2: Minor Fouls

dangerous play	high kicking near another player's head or trying to play a ball held by the goalkeeper
fair charging	using your shoulder by leaning against the shoulder of an opponent to push him or her off balance so you can get the ball when the ball is more than four feet away from you
illegal obstruction	a player intentionally gets between the ball and an opponent when not within playing distance of the ball
charging the goalkeeper	shoulder-to-shoulder contact within the penalty area
goalkeeper steps	goalkeeper taking more than four steps while controlling the ball with his or her hands

Dangerous play is considered one of the five minor fouls.

Who Calls the Fouls?

The referee is in charge during a soccer game. It is the referee's job to oversee the safety of the players. The referee calls the fouls.

Soccer is one of the few sports where the referee can decide whether to call a foul or not. If the referee feels that calling a foul will hurt the fouled team, he may decide not to call it.

The referee calls the fouls during a soccer game.

Offside

There is one more important soccer rule you should know about. It is called **offside**, and it means being ahead of the ball when it is played in your direction. To be called offside, you must be in your opponent's half of the field and have fewer than two opponents ahead of you when the ball is played to you by a teammate.

If a player is called offside, the opposing team is awarded an indirect free kick. Do you remember the difference between indirect and direct free kicks? If not, go back and reread the sections that describe each of these important penalty kicks.

Equipment

You do not need much equipment to play soccer. If you are playing with friends, all you really need is a soccer ball. If you are playing on a team, shinguards are required for games and strongly suggested for practices. Shinguards protect the front part of the leg below the knee and above the ankle. Many shinguards also have a cup made of teflon to protect the ankle.

Soccer shoes are not required but can be important. The soft cleats on the bottom of the shoes help prevent slipping. The sturdy construction of the shoes also provides extra foot support.

Some soccer coaches suggest using long shoelaces. They instruct their players to wrap the laces around the arch of the shoe. This, they say, helps support the foot when you kick the ball.

Most AYSO soccer teams play in uniforms (shirt, shorts, and socks) supplied by the local region. The local region also supplies field equipment (goals, nets, and flags).

Shinguards are required safety gear when playing on a team.

The soft cleats on soccer shoes can help prevent slipping and falling.

"Be A Good Sport"

The AYSO has its own "Be A Good Sport" program. The program defines good behavior for players, coaches, and parents on and off the field. Whether you play on an AYSO team or with friends, it is always a good idea to be a good sport.

Being a good sport means treating other players as you would like to be treated. It means playing by the rules and playing for fun. A good sport never argues with the referee or with the coach. A good sport controls his or her temper. A good sport does not show off, but works as a member of a team.

Whether winning or losing, it's important to be a good sport.

Pele´ was a famous soccer player born in Brazil.

CONCLUSION

Soccer is one of the most popular games in the world today. It is becoming one of America's favorite sports, too. More and more young people learn to play the game each year. Professional soccer teams represent many American cities.

You have probably heard of a man called Pelé. He was a famous soccer player. He was also the best paid athlete in his time. Pelé's real name is Edson Arantes Do Nascimento. He was born in Brazil in 1940. Pelé led the Brazilian national soccer team to World Cup victories in 1958, 1962, and 1970.

On November 20, 1969, Pelé scored his 1,000th goal. He became a Brazilian national hero! Pelé is a medium-sized man. He is 5 feet 8 inches tall and weighs 160 pounds. He combined kicking power and accuracy to become a great soccer player. He also had the ability to predict when and where other players were going to move.

Pelé retired from soccer in 1974. But in 1975, he agreed to play with the New York Cosmos soccer team for three years. His goal was to help make soccer popular here in the United States.

Many young soccer players dream of playing like Pelé. He was a soccer great. Who knows? If you give the game your best, you too may become a famous soccer player.

GLOSSARY

arc - the quarter circle at each corner of the field in which the ball is placed for a corner kick

attacking - the team that has the ball and is trying to score a point

charge - shoulder-to-shoulder contact or running into an opponent from behind

chip pass - a short kick over an opponent's head to a teammate

corner kick - a kick taken from an arc by the attacking team when the defending team last touched the ball before it crossed the goal line and went out of bounds

defender - a player whose main job is to stop the opponent from having a good shot at the goal

defensive team - the team that does not have the ball; job is to stop the attacking team from scoring

direct free kick - a free kick awarded to a team when the opposing team commits one of nine major fouls

dribbling - moving the ball with the foot by repeatedly kicking it short distances

forward - a player whose main job is to score

foul - an illegal play or movement by a player

goal - one point awarded to the attacking team when the ball goes between the goal posts, under the crossbar, and over the goal line

goalkeeper - the player whose main job is to stop the ball from going into the goal; the only player who can use his or her hands

goal kick - a free kick for the defending team when the attacking team kicks the ball across the goal line and out of bounds

goal line - the line where the goal posts stand across each end of the field

goal posts - the posts that hold up the crossbar

half-line - the line across the middle of the field that divides it in half

heading - hitting the ball with the forehead

indirect free kick - a free kick given to a team when the opposing team commits one of the five minor fouls

kicking - kicking at an opponent

kickoff - puts the ball in motion at the beginning of each half and after each goal is scored

midfielder (halfback) - player who plays both offense and defense in the middle of the field

offside - a penalty called when a player is ahead of the ball in the opponent's half of the field with fewer than two opponents ahead of him or her

offensive team - the team that has control of the ball

out of play - the ball crosses the sideline or the goal line of the field

passing - kicking, pushing, or heading the ball to a teammate or to a space where a teammate can run to the ball

penalty - a free shot at the goal

penalty box - the lines that form the rectangle within which the goalkeeper may use his or her hands to touch the ball

penalty kick - a free kick at the goal inside the penalty area

referee - the person whose main job is the safety of the players; calls penalties and decides whether goals have been scored legally

throw-in - throwing the ball onto the field from the sideline at the point where the ball went out of play; awarded against the team that last touched the ball

trapping - stopping the ball in flight or on the ground and then controlling it